N THE DARK, MOVE SLOWLY

IN THE DARK,
MOVE SLOWLY

Tuomas Anhava

Poems
selected and translated
from the Finnish
by
Anselm Hollo

CAPE GOLIARD PRESS LONDON
In Association with
GROSSMAN PUBLISHERS NEW YORK

All the originals of the poems translated here are contained in:
"Tuomas Anhava, *Runot 1951–1966*" published by Otava,
Helsinki, 1967.

Some of these translations have appeared in BLUE PIG
(Paris), CONTEMPORARY LITERATURE IN
TRANSLATION (Toronto), POOR.OLD.TIRED.
HORSE (Edinburgh), STAND QUARTERLY
(Newcastle-on-Tyne), TLALOC (Leeds), and
WAYSGOOSE (Oxford).

Cover photograph by C. A. Breyer.

Tuomas Anhava:

Born 1927.

A master, of his time place language: of the short poem, epigram, tanka, haiku – and of the *ode*, a form having remarkable contemporary practitioners in Northumbrian and American poetry: Basil Bunting, Charles Olson, Frank O'Hara, Charles Boer.

Like at least three of those men, a master, mentor, of two generations of younger poets in his time place language.

Translator of Ezra Pound, Cavafy, others; critic, active anthologist publisher. Man who eats drinks / wakes and sleeps with poetry, nevertheless also lives in a time place language that is *shared*, "from eight to six".

Hoping he is here now, in *this* time place language

Anselm Hollo
Iowa City,
April 1969

ELEGY
FOR THE NIGHT

The night I love
but the days I have married,
the day talks, my wife repeats it
the day makes a mess, my wife cleans it up
the street is loud, like of flock of children.

But the night, o the night. Her face, not to be seen
only felt, and it is soft: her hair
rustling like leaves, her speech, a wind
without words,
and her eyes beckon
like streetlamps, to say nothing
of the stars.

WITH, THESE, CONCEPTS

Today, and always, may death be remembered.
By moments we are killed, little by little: we are
because there is, a little, to lose, that is, all
we have; for others
we are but mirrors, our words do not reach them
but are transformed into thoughts, their thoughts;
let our love
be silent. Ourselves
we look for, in others, and tire of it
but a little, by moments,
moment by moment is used, and worn away,
our one, only, all, our self, its loss
is the way, is the life, is what truth there is.

THE BIRDS

When a bird goes
        it is different
when a bird goes
        it is a light fall
when a bird goes
        it is an easy flight
when a bird goes
        it is quite different

from the departure of one dead: he drags himself
away, crumbles onto the road, piecemeal,
and nothing remains to be buried but his corpse.

When a bird comes
        it is quite different
when a bird comes
        it is light knuckles on the door
when a bird comes
        it is a foot stepping lightly away
when a bird comes
        it is different

from the arrival of one dead: in pain, he is removed
from the dying, a cry, from the cry —
out, onto the road, from the dust, to dust.

IN THE TWILIGHT

The child fell asleep
and its smile followed it into sleep,
curled up in the shadow
cast by one cheek.

You slept,
a shadow of grief on your brow.

I am awake
              and the smile, always new
              the grief, always forever
rises into my eyes

and I see it is dusk and dawn,
my night, my day
between the two of them.

All these days I have been looking at the sky.
A great deal of grey. Many shades of grey.

The darkness feels good now. I wait for it to be time,
for things to come to a stop   in the sky.

the dragonfly
sun on its wings

scissoring scissoring
the air

won't shift an inch from its place
above the stream

I come and I
go.

Harder
and harder

to say any
word.

From eight to six,
eight to six.
I don't know my children anymore.

Many's the time when the trees were blowing
the trees were blowing and the air flew
below me and past, many's the time
I then thought of
                    the wing
            folding back, yes, thus
of flying,
            the act
                    as air and trees
and wings,
                they
                    folded back and I fell
a Philosopher's Stone, I fell, in the act,
                    even deeper
                        still deeper I then
thought of
            flying, like this:
unfold the wings (and the tail),
            forward and down and up from
                the back, a beat and a beat,
that simple –
                then
                        I thought how
                simple it is, and how treacherous
for if flight
                    needs wings, it is not
perfect, no no, not
                        universally
                        applicable, no, not worth it
(and the tail:
how do the tailless fare in that case and where
are the wingless
then),
            and if
it needs air it isn't true flight at all
at all,
            if it requires
                        beating the air
it is

in fact, in the act, a worthless
diacatalectical
spectacle
          between the
          heights
          and the
          depths,
thesis of wing
                    to antithesis of air
the synthesis, is it
                    flight?
I then thought, and my thoughts
ever deeper, all the way down to Germany
and I grew weary and fell asleep, yes, thus
with open eyes,
                    and the wings
                              opened out
          and the air
– in an instant, the air
                    rushed below and above and by
and the earth (which is tailless)
                    stretched out and flew,
                                        it flew wherever
          a flying carpet
and, the trees, oh
counter-clockwise
                    blew and the air flew
sky's ceiling drew ever higher, closer
the clouds, the rain-bellied, radiant-backed
                    looked on, looked on
                    without moving, as if in a storm
my eyes
were open too, like this:
yes flying
          flying, the act, the metaphor
the image
in the air

1962: CHANDOGYA

Under my feet, the floor, and under the floor, an apartment
and under that apartment, an apartment, and an apartment,
down below, under those, the main central heating,
and under that, always, the building lot.
In one wall there are two windows, in two walls there are doors,
two walls of books, a floor and a table,
a chair and a low wooden bench.
In the morning the sun shines, at night the lamp is lit.
Above my head is the ceiling, above that, the loft,
above the loft there's the roof, on the roof, an aerial, on the aerial

I have become a resident of this building
and my time here is like the city,
very quiet,
the days drone past steadily in the street's ravine,
with swallows sparrows seagulls wind in the air
and when the sky darkens to match the rooftops' colour
each set of footsteps is suddenly audible,
then fades

Harder to remain calm, when the silence grows
I said, I have said it already, I have nothing
but a restless mind,
at a loss
here I am *l'entre deux morts*
        and all of a sudden I want to see how it is
        when my son's face lights up in a smile
        from just one little word

Never have I been able to concentrate
on any one thing
                one understanding
                        one hatred

The world shrinks and increases in density,
blessings and temptations draw closer to one another,
the victories and losses of justice grow terrible and enormous.
I do not admit, I do not deny, I do not give in.
Keep my eyes open
                    not understanding much
people and books
                open up
          like those windows in the wall
                                        into worlds.
The fearless voice will not die: Chandogya
                        The fearless voice will not die

          Windows, the colour of fish-scales, gaping like guns:
          the schoolhouse in the evening,
                                        a symbol.

Remember to believe,
remember to turn and bow down
facing the place where you know
                                for certain
                there is no one there.

MAY, 1964

I

A night in May, in the May of nights
out of the day gone west into the sea
out of the day, and sweet now, with an offshore wind,
smoke rising out of the ship,
sails of darkness, remote islands,
star-studded masts and shores and horizons,
northern,
budding forth from the cold,
a youth, a maiden
and the tree's maidenhair rustle so green! so light!
the earth, now moist and open,
May, gone now,
time without time
of the northern night,
high, leisurely, a migrant hawk
gliding at twilight speed
a waking dream
and the dew on the roads
stretching towards the morning and the city,
morning, holding its breath
rooftops, mirrors
ablaze like the open sea
a youth as old as the sun
everything held
in its eyes,
the true, the green, the grey
the eyes, gazing far out to sea;
wind on the forehead
and transience,
proud as a ship

II

The moments, like statues, and the statue

  its eyes blinded by distance
  its breath becalmed
  the marble heartbeat within the ribcage
  the hand's gesture, casting no shadow
  the frozen step
  the elegance of nudity

incontrovertible as dreams
as youth, there is no return
who would not find it beautiful
to die into memory
to be forgotten eternally

when youth dies
it makes us feel so immortal

III

Who is young, who would go
would do every thing, everywhere
say this and say that, meet others, always in new frames of mind,
then sleep, in his sleep, in a peace of this world.
Not having acquired that skill of statues, spectators
of freezing into stillness,
for a moment it takes your breath away, eternity,
then gives it back,
it is not in the fire, but the flesh is alive,
it has its desires, its fears, it is at one with all living creatures,
whenever the sky is ablaze, the sea rises, the wind
touches his forehead
and transience, a message: the heat of crematoria.
His pores are open, the world moves in and out
in him who is young, most alive, most mortal,
but we know that our peace is anguished
and this certainty makes him uncertain, this skill makes him
clumsy,
wealth impoverishes, cleanliness soils him
and our shame forces him to avert his face,
this labour, so productive, yet so useless in so many ways
makes his heart sink, and the freedom he is permitted
turns into anxiety in his mind,
our dwellings force him out into the street.
One sees a migrant hawk and decides to follow it, into
extinction.
But most of them follow us, well, what about us;
some follow those who do not want anything any more,
who don't even want to die, members of no class,
there aren't many of them, anywhere, there are a few everywhere,
a harmless amount of activity, in our bones.
Who would not like to set his course the way youth does,
the cunning radical, the middle-aged, the jovial bishop at the
bazaar,

and old age, guided by right and might and reality, faith
and beauty and terror, all the sisters of our dreams
and finally, always, indifference,
the sister no one invited.
Not a springtime, no sea, no creature
left unpoisoned. And it is only twenty years, now.
We ask what is going on, the world replies,
it is all of it going on, it is, all of it, real.
No one would like to wait for that answer.
The songs have died. I grieve,
grieve for Scylla and grieve for Charybdis,
both of them sirens, both of them choked to death.

IV

The immortals? I do not think of them often.
I think of the others, all the others
one cannot remember, only consider,
cannot imagine, only know. The mortal ones,
more and more often I think of them. *Manes et maiores.*
Just names, if that. Dates, if that,
but years, yes, endlessly, years. Gone with their days
and with those who did remember,
if they ever had any of those.

But not as you would think of a procession,
of some frieze of anonymous exaltation.
Among them, perhaps,
        an old man who kept telling his ailments like a rosary.
        A difficult child, subnormal, pacified with cold water.
        The nurse who told me about it and smiled.
        The polite young man who had a few rare words in
                                            his vocabulary.
        Two women who used to read their newspaper every
                            day, from the first to the last page.
Workers idlers finger-tappers talkers runts gluttons blondes
                            pedants hotheads rawbones.
From morning without morning
until night without night – see, there you are,
even you can be buried under a phrase.
Farewell
Goodbye
We'll come as soon as

V

The last day of May
of the last May?
the invisibility of tomorrow
but this May is pushing its leaves into June
in the morning, the rock dove
covered in dust, turned its head, trembling
the sun was out, the air was blue to breathe
the sun is still out, the air is bright
and in the midst of this day, this pay-day, the daily reckoning
I appear in the doorway of the Bank
suddenly filled with wonder at all that goes on
with tenderness
the women! the women, like perennials
the men like wardrobes
their steps in the street
the sun is out, howl of cars
trams lorries ignorant armies
  If rain has fallen,
   where will our nostrils meet with the scent of that grove?
   how does the twig lie across the path?
   where does the cloud go? when there is no one there
   and what is blue?
I go in through the door
the lift squeaks to a stop, the doors slam
the world is a city and does not cease
these rooms where I live receive it, the surge of the surge
  What did you say? it does not cease?
  and suddenly all is quiet:
   sometimes, it is.
And that, too, is received here,
through the open window.
Then you hear it again. Someone whistling.
A boy. Down in the yard. No tune.
Just whistling. His own.

Murdering
four mice – too much
for my conscience. It was. I
murdered them.
They had come when I'd known how to sit there,
                 calmly, just right,
they had run, trying to get away
their hind legs slipping and sprawling,
                  brought tears to my eyes.

I thought how each
                    tree, house, man
stands apart when there is no one to see them

            Such a *callous* thrill
when plant roots tangle and grope the Earth

And is there a sky; and what does it feel like
                    if one is a horse

I am the truth of my dreams

a dream,
            not for your eyes

and
intermittent.

Again   as then
everything grows huge
the whirr of the fan
I am   and not

Feel cold
would not   do not
want to speak about it
me
and there is
wine and bread on the table for me

That mouth
won't open   ever
mouth out of your mouth
and mine
it was then that I began to die
and now it is
soon over
we do not meet in him who was to come
for ever   we are removed from each other

Having a sad time
in a forestful of wind
one morning
I wake up
remember my father's name
times houses islands
soft childhood waters

I want to be
                    with you
want myself into you
away from this place
now
        right now

This night
one more
once more
these trees
are green
the sun
sets
back of the sky

This glimpse
under the curtain's hem
that rustling sound
that bird
voice breaks
time and again
(monotonous)

Once more
this night
these thoughts
this heaviness
once more
to sleep
through this one

My hand

open

you come to mind

to the mind
in my fingers

How he gets to me now,
      Zeus

            Leda, the swan

as slowly suddenly everything
      turns lovely
                  under my hand

is a high downy bird-cry
      is a shiver

            is huge, wings

Small night talk with you:
    the children have settled down

Then, it's an owl
    calling
        loud and clear

another
    answering

The rain's confused chatter, the child's babble
rock me to sleep in the long stories I read to my sons,
            the rain makes them restless,
my breath evens out, I go out of myself

the whole long memory of the rainy day revives in me
and I remember the rock I used to lie on,
full of consciousness, of pain.

My son came to me, he was troubled,
I said something absurd, and he laughed;
his laugh cut straight through the tears
and the weeping entered into me, the one who knows.

Everyone who believes what he sees
                is a mystic.
In the dark
            move slowly.

I do not remember.
Summer
            like a woman against my skin.
It is November.
                It has gone.

This first edition was designed, printed and
published by Cape Goliard Press, 10a Fairhazel
Gardens London N.W.6.

Printed in Great Britain.